The Many Colors of The Master's Plan

A COLORING BOOK

Illustrated by

DiAne Gates

Scripture taken from the NEW AMERICAN STANDARD BIBLE®,

Copyright © 1960, 1962, 1963, 1968, 1971, 1972, 1973, 1975, 1977, 1995 by The Lockman Foundation. Used by permission.

Published in the United States of America

God gifted me with an eye to see and a hand to draw and paint. I rely on Him, my family, and the beauty of life for inspiration to play across my keyboard, paper, and canvas. A native Floridian—sea, salt, and sand rub between my toes.

For those who've read *The Master's Plan Revealed Through Creation,* first book in this series was dedicated to my three grandchildren, with a not so subtle hint about great grandchildren...God hears and answers prayers!

Right this moment, MASON GABRIEL FLORES, first-born of Kalyn and Vittorio Flores, is being woven together in his mother's womb! And this precious baby boy is our first great grandchild. *The Many Colors of the Master's Plan* is dedicated to you, sweet Mason. What a blessing all of you are in my life! And what a marvelous journey each of you are about to begin!

Mimi

¹⁴ Let the words of my mouth
and the meditation of my heart
Be acceptable in Your sight,
O Lord, my rock and
my Redeemer.

Psalm 19:14 (NASB)

¹ In the beginning God created the heavens and the earth.

Genesis 1:1 (NASB)

²⁷ *Depart from evil and do good,*
So you will abide forever.

Psalm 37:27 (NASB)

*¹² Blessed is the nation whose
God is the Lord,
The people whom He has chosen
for His own inheritance.*

Psalm 33:12 (NASB)

¹¹ For He will give His angels
charge concerning you,
To guard you in all your ways.

Psalm 91:11 (NASB)

*34 I will bless the Lord at all times;
His praise shall continually be in
my mouth.*

PSALM 34:1 (NASB)

⁶ Splendor and majesty are before Him, Strength and beauty are in His sanctuary.

Psalm 96:6 (NASB)

¹³ *I set My bow in the cloud, and it shall be for a sign of a covenant between Me and the earth.*

Genesis 9:13 (NASB)

7 The fear of the Lord is the beginning of knowledge; Fools despise wisdom and instruction.

Proverbs 1:7 (NASB)

¹³ With my lips I have told of All the ordinances of Your mouth.

Psalm 119:13 (NASB)

89 *Forever, O Lord,*
Your word is settled in heaven.

Psalm 119:89 (NASB)

¹⁹ *And He said to them, "Follow Me, and I will make you fishers of men."*

Matthew 4:19 (NASB)

⁴ And He answered and said, "Have you not read that He who created them from the beginning made them male and female…

Matthew 19:4 (NASB)

3 Trust in the Lord and do good; Dwell in the land and cultivate faithfulness.

Psalm 37:3 (NASB)

¹⁸ If I regard wickedness in my heart, The Lord will not hear;

Psalm 66:18 (NASB)

²⁶ *Give thanks to the God of heaven, For His loving kindness is everlasting.*

Psalm 136:26 (NASB)

[1] Children obey your parents in the Lord, for this is right."

Ephesians 6:1 (NASB)

14 You are My friends if you do what I command you.

John 15:14 (NASB)

⁹ I will give thanks to You, O Lord, among the peoples; I will sing praises to You among the nations.

Psalm 57:9 (NASB)

¹⁶ *Your eyes have seen my unformed substance; And in Your book were all written The days that were ordained for me, When as yet there was not one of them.*

Psalm 139:16 (NASB)

ABOUT THE AUTHOR

DiAne Gates writes Christian fiction for children, YA, and non-fiction for adults through her blogs:

http://dianegates.wordpress.com/ and www.floridagirlturnedtexan.wordpress.com

Freelance artist and photographer, she facilitates GriefShare, an international support group for people struggling through the loss of a loved one.

This first book in her four book Master Plan Series, *The Master's Plan: Revealed Through Creation*, will be followed with Book 2, *The Master's Plan: Revealed Through His Word (Spring 2020)*, then Book 3, *The Master's Plan: Revealed Through the Life of the Master (Fall 2020)* and Book 4, *The Master's Plan: Revealed Through You (early 2021)*.

DiAne's award-winning, western adventure series, *ROPED*, released August of 2015, and the second book, *TWISTED*, released by Pelican Book Group in July of 2017. Her third book in this series, *UNTIED*, is a work-in-progress.

Wife, mother, Mimi, and child of the Living God, whose passion is to share those hard life lessons God allows to conform us to the image of His Son.

Find DiAne on Facebook at DiAne Gates or look for her books on Amazon.

Made in the USA
Monee, IL
13 April 2020